The Real Facts of Life

Practical Reflections on the Three Marks of Existence

Sumano Tong

Buddhist Publication Society
Kandy • Sri Lanka

Published in 2000

Buddhist Publication Society
P.O. Box 61
54, Sangharaja Mawatha
Kandy, Sri Lanka

Copyright © 2000 by Sumano Tong Tuck Sung

ISBN 955–24–0205–0

Printed in Sri Lanka by
Karunaratne & Sons Ltd.
67 U.D.A., Industrial Estate
Katuwana
Homagama

THE WHEEL PUBLICATION NO. 435

Dedicated to my precious teachers,
who taught me the sublime Dhamma:

the late Mr. T.A. Simon

the late Ven. Nārada Mahāthera

Introduction

The Buddha taught that all conditioned things – ourselves included – have three characteristics: impermanence (*anicca*), unsatisfactoriness (*dukkha*), and selflessness or non-substantiality (*anattā*). When we fail to recognize these three characteristics of existence, we regard that which is impermanent as permanent, that which is unsatisfactory as pleasure, and the selfless as possessing an unchanging self.

The Buddha summed up these tendencies in the Pali word *avijjā*, ignorance. Being ignorant of our own true nature, and of the true nature of the things around us, we engage in actions based on these delusions, and thereby we accumulate kamma which keeps us in bondage to the cycle of birth and death.

It is through understanding these characteristics that wisdom arises. Only then can one free oneself from the bonds of rebirth and attain Nibbāna, the permanent end of suffering.

The following article is a humble attempt to analyse the three characteristics of existence based on day-to-day observations. It makes no pretense at erudition or mastery of the scriptures. By reflecting on my own daily experience, and on the experiences of others, I have jotted down various pointers to the three characteristics in facts and events lying just beneath our noses. I hope these reflections will help you, too, to see the truth of the Dhamma more clearly in your own everyday life.

I
Analysis of Anicca

What is the meaning of the word "*anicca*"?
The Pali word "*anicca*" means impermanent.

What is impermanent?
One is oneself impermanent, both physically and mentally, and all conditioned things around one are impermanent.

In what way is one's physical body impermanent?

Posture
One's posture is constantly being changed from one of the following to another: sitting, standing, walking, and lying down.

State of health
One's health is ever fluctuating depending on many factors. Some days one feels well, other days one feels ill; some days one feels energetic, other days one feels weak.

Cleanliness
Immediately after the body is cleaned, it gradually becomes soiled again due to the secretion of skin grease and sweat and due to contact with pollutants in the environment.

Growth and decay

The hair of one's head and one's nails are constantly increasing in length; body hairs are constantly falling off and being replaced; the skin of the whole body is constantly being shed and worn away; the body cells are always being replaced; one's body mass (weight) is ever fluctuating; the whole body is gradually ageing and one day it will die.

Nutrients for the Body

The air that one breathes in is being converted to carbon dioxide. The water one drinks is converted to sweat and urine. Within a day the food one eats turns into faeces.

In what way is *one's mind* impermanent?

Feeling

One's bodily sensations alternate between pleasure and pain, hunger and fullness, thirst and satiation.

One's mental feelings vary between pleasure, displeasure, and indifference, depending on many factors, such as the sense object one experiences.

One's state of mind is ever changing from one to another: joyful, angry, sad, happy, bored, worried, greedy, faithful, etc.

One's interests change as one grows older.

One's perceptions of the things around oneself also change with time or with one's age, e.g., one's choice of colours, one's preference for type of material or design, or one's opinion about an issue.

In what way are the *things around one* impermanent?

All human artifacts (houses, buildings, bridges, roads, cars, etc.) gradually get soiled by the dirt in the environment, wither due to exposure to ultra-violet rays from the sun, and get eroded by chemical laden rain. Due to wear and tear, some day the mechanism of such objects will cease to function.

Things in vogue
Due to the advancement in science and technology, their designs, materials, and methods of use change with time. These changes apply to all human artifacts.

Flowers
bloom, wither, and decay.

Fruits
ripen, fall off the tree, and decay.

Trees
constantly shed their bark and seasonally shed their leaves.

Grass in the fields
is constantly being replaced by younger blades of grass.

All sentient life forms
are gradually ageing and being replaced by their offspring. Daily a large number of species are becoming extinct.

Hills , mountains, and plains
are ever rising and sinking, usually imperceptibly, due to geological processes such as faulting, folding, large scale uplift, and volcanic activity.

Rivers
are always flowing and their waters are ever changing. They either widen, become narrower, dry up during a drought, or overflow during a flood. Their shapes and directions change with the passage of time.

The seas
Their water is gradually converted into clouds and the clouds send down rain, which again enters the seas. The tide is alternating between high and low tides. The sea bed is ever rising or sinking, though very slowly.

The sky
is constantly changing its colour morning, noon, afternoon, evening, and night. Its appearance is constantly changing depending on the weather, and is different on sunny, clear, cloudy, and rainy days. The positions of the sun, moon, all other planets, clouds, and stars are ever changing.

The sun
is always changing its composition, and scientists are convinced that some day it will burn out, just as millions of other stars have expired or are expiring this very moment.

The moon
constantly alternates between its waxing and waning phases.

The seasons
constantly change from spring to summer, summer to autumn, autumn to winter, and winter to spring again.

Food
immediately after being prepared gradually starts to decay or to grow stale.

II
Analysis of Dukkha

What is the meaning of the word "*dukkha*"?
The Pali word "*dukkha*" is often translated as suffering, unsatisfactoriness, pain, or sorrow. It encompass all unpleasantness, from the slightest uneasiness to unbearable torment.

In what way is one subject to suffering?
Suffering can be physical, mental, or a combination of both.
1. We must be reborn over and over again, and *birth* is suffering.
2. After one is born, one is always liable to fall ill, and *illness* is suffering.
3. After we have passed the prime of youth, our vitality starts to decline and we begin to grow old. *Old age* is suffering.
4. We must face inevitable *death*, and that is suffering.
5. To *associate with the unpleasant* is suffering.
6. To be *separated from the pleasant* is suffering.
7. *Not to have one's wishes fulfilled* is suffering.
8. The *composite body* itself is a cause of suffering.

In what way is *birth* suffering?
Birth leads to old age, sickness, and death as well as to all other kinds of suffering.

In what way is *sickness* suffering?

One's liability to sickness is itself a cause of suffering, for we often worry about falling ill.

When we do fall ill, the illness may be short-termed, chronic, or life-threatening.

Short-termed illness

We suffer *physically* when experiencing any of the following: fever, chill, ache, pain, nausea, vomiting, diarrhoea, constipation, giddiness, weakness of the limbs, cough, running nose, itchiness, sore throat, sprain, fracture, insomnia, loss of appetite, cuts and abrasions, piles and fissures.

We suffer *mentally* when our wish, "May this sickness quickly pass" is not fulfilled.

Chronic illness

We suffer *physically* when we contract such diseases as diabetes, kidney failure, heart condition, bronchitis, arthritis, Parkinson's disease, Lupus, hepatitis, etc.

We suffer *mentally* worrying that the sickness might worsen, or when the wish, "May I be permanently cured of this illness" is not fulfilled.

Life threatening and degenerative illnesses

The *physical* suffering we undergo is dependent on the type of illness – such as cancer, AIDS, etc. – but illness always brings bodily suffering.

We suffer *mentally* knowing that there is little hope of recovery and that our days are numbered. We suffer even more when anticipating permanent separation from our loved ones.

Evidence for anxiety about health and longevity

We are extra careful in selecting the food we eat and prefer food low in salt, sugar, and cholesterol content, free from artificial colouring and preservatives, but high in fibre and enriched with minerals.

We make regular visits to the health-food shop to purchase vitamins, bee pollen, calcium supplements, garlic pills, cod liver oil, bird's nests, Ganoderma (Ling Zhi), ginseng root and ginseng extracts, all sorts of herbs and herbal extracts, and other nutritional supplements.

We install drinking water filters and air purifiers in our homes.

We visit the oxygen bar to breathe in 95 percent concentrated oxygen.

We buy health enhancing equipment such as massaging chairs and devices, exercise bicycles, tread mills, rowing machines and various instruments for measuring blood pressure, blood glucose, pulse rate, cholesterol level, etc.

We go to the doctor for regular medical checkups and health screening.

We seek physical treatments such as massage therapy and foot reflexology, healing by crystals and stones, etc.

We attend health promoting meditation sessions.

We subscribe to tele-medical services.

In what way is *ageing* suffering?

Degeneration of one's physical appearance

Our hair thins and turns grey, our hairline recedes, our skin dries and wrinkles, pigmented spots appear on our skin, our shoulders start to droop and our spine bends, our muscles turn flabby, bags appear under our eyes, our cheeks and eyelids sag, our teeth turn yellow or become chipped and we start to lose our teeth, our face loses its youthful lustre, our eyes and hair become dull, our nails are discoloured, when we smile wrinkles form on our face.

Gradual failing of one's sense faculties

Eyes
We are unable to see distant objects or fine details of nearby objects. We must make use of eyeglasses.

Ears
We are unable to hear soft sounds, and become sensitive to loud noises. We become dependent on a hearing aid.

Nose
Our sensitivity to odours is reduced.

Tongue
We lose our appreciation of tastes.

Degeneration of our bodily structure
Our teeth become weak and brittle; our bones become porous and brittle, increasing our vulnerability to fractures; our joints loosen, increasing our vulnerability to sprains. Weaker bones and muscles mean clumsiness in our movements, pains in our joints, and other frailties.

Degeneration of bodily functions
We have to undergo reduced endurance in physical activities such as prolonged walking due to lack of stamina; reduced general flexibility and agility resulting in slower

responses and reflexes; reduced capability in weight-bearing tasks such as carrying heavy objects; lowered resistance to microbes and viruses; longer recovery period after sickness or injury; difficulty in falling asleep and shorter span of sleep.

The unfortunate contract illnesses such as senile dementia, incontinence, and Parkinson's disease.

Men need a longer time to urinate due to the gradual enlargement of the prostrate gland as a result of ageing.

Women stop menstrating while men need a longer time to achieve erection.

Gradual degeneration of the mental faculties
Memory fades more quickly and concentration becomes weaker. Studies show that the ageing brain may to some extent lose its depth perception and have more difficulty in locating objects in space or in quickly identifying geometric shapes.

The things people do to camouflage ageing
They blacken their hair with dyes; undergo plastic surgery to remove wrinkles and bags under their eyes; use various skin moisturizers to hide the signs of ageing; use spectacles with bifocal lenses (but without parting lines); seek regular youth enhancement injections; whiten their teeth with polish or by chemical or laser treatment; get dentures to replace missing teeth; apply facial cosmetics to emulate the lost lustre of youth.

Some take new anti-ageing compounds aimed at the symptoms of ageing, such as: anti-impotence treatment (Viagra), bone density regulators, baldness remedies, Ginkyo Bilboa for the brain, African tree bark to pump up the libido, Saw Palmetto for the prostrate, chelated minerals and amino acids for energy, youth hormones (dehydroepi-andsterone or DHEA), etc.

In what way is *death* suffering?

Death is suffering due to:
One's fear of physical suffering at the time of death.
One's fear of mental suffering at the dying moment.
One's misery over being permanently separated from one's loved ones.
One's fear of the unknown beyond death.

The suffering of death is more intense when one dies in the prime of youth, or when one is enjoying success in one's education or career; or when one is rich, powerful and famous; or when one is enjoying a happy family with a caring spouse and lovely children.

From the Buddhist standpoint, death is suffering because it leads to rebirth, which entails a renewal of the whole mass of suffering.

In what way is *association with the unpleasant* suffering?

People
It is painful to work with inconsiderate or uncooperative colleagues; to be subordinate to an excessively demanding or unreasonable superior; to have an apathetic or dishonest business partner; to live next to inconsiderate neighbours; to be married to an unsuitable spouse; to witness strained relations between one's spouse and one's parents and family members.

Places

It is unpleasant to be born in a place where the basic requisites of food, clothing, medicine, and shelter are scarce or not easily available.

It is unpleasant to dwell in an uncomfortable environment, one which is eerie, hazardous, badly coloured, poorly ventillated; too bright or too dark; too quiet or too noisy; too dry or too humid; too warm or too cold; stinking and polluted; or when the contacting surfaces are filthy, sticky, slippery, too hard, too rough, irregular; or when there are obstacles to movement and physical constraints, etc.

It is unpleasant to dwell in a place infested with pests such as cockroaches, lizards, and rats.

It is unpleasant to live in proximity to harmful and ferocious animals such as lions, tigers, snakes, scorpions, and crocodiles.

It is unpleasant to live in a politically unstable country where one's life is constantly at risk.

It is unpleasant to have to live in a place where one's livelihood is dependent on unreliable conditions or where destructive natural forces may unexpectedly strike; for example, in the form of drought, famine, floods, locusts, rodents, or any other pests.

It is unpleasant to live in a place affected by climatic phenomena such as El Nino, La Nina, the greenhouse effect, the ozone hole.

It is unpleasant to live in a place frequently struck by floods, mudslides, hailstorms, droughts, forest fires, heat waves, hurricanes, cyclones, tornados, tidal waves, and volcano eruptions.

It is upleasant to live in a place affected by dense electronic radiation, smog, or polluted air.

Events

It is stressful to be awaiting the outcome of an attempt to rescue a loved one involved in a disaster; to sit for an examination; to attend a job interview; to give an important presentation before a group of superiors; to have to meet important people; to await the results of a medical test for a critical diagnosis; to lose one's job; to undergo a marital separation or divorce.

It is stressful to work long hours to meet deadlines, with no alternative. It is also stressful to take on more than one job in order to make ends meet.

Stressful moments particularly for the young include: their first date with a member of the opposite sex; their first meeting with their future parents-in-law; awaiting the arrival of a baby, etc.

In what way is *separation from the pleasant* suffering?

People

Temporary separation such as having to leave one's loved ones for another country to pursue further studies or career.

Permanent separation due to the death of a loved one.

Being abandoned by one's siblings.

Places

Having to leave the place of work which one considered pleasant due to the expiry of one's contract; leaving a country which one considered pleasant due to immigration laws.

Objects

The death of a pet, or the breakage or loss of a favourite object.

In what way is it suffering *not to have one's wishes fulfilled*?

Appearance
Most men would like to be handsome, tall, with a muscular body; most women would like to be beautiful, tall, with an attractive figure. Yet only a very small minority obtain such qualities.

Everyone would like to be free from physical defects, yet some are born with a disfigured face, limbs, and body. Some are hairless, hare-lipped, or with defective sexual organs. Some have unsighty birthmarks, skin discolouration, foul body odour, bad breath, sweaty palms, a rough voice, pimples, freckles, rough skin, unsighty body hairs, etc.

Some of the things men and women do to enhance their looks
Attend grooming courses; seek facial treatments; use cosmetics and perfumes; take up body building or aerobic exercises; whiten their teeth and replace unsighty teeth with dentures; fill dental cavities with porcelain (instead of metal); use contact lenses; dye their hair; wear abdominal bands; undergo surgery for jaw-line correction; wear wigs or resort to hair transplants or herbal massages for baldness.

Some of the things women do to improve their looks
Participate in slimming programmes; perm their hair; take treatment for wrinkles, freckles, or pigment problems; undergo surgery such as double eyelids creation; insert artificial body implants such as nose bridges and silicon breasts; liposuction; wear push-up brassiere; tattoo their eyebrows; body and limb wraps; mud or herbal baths; manicures; re-align teeth with braces; wear high-heeled shoes;

wear clothes with shoulder pads; stick on artificial fingernails and eye lashes.

Health

Everyone hopes to be healthy throughout their lives, but not all are blessed with health. Various illnesses to which one is subject have been enumerated above. Besides one's own infirmity, one also experiences intense suffering when a loved one becomes critically ill and can only survive by receiving a bone-marrow transplant, or a platelets transfusion, or a blood transfusion of a rare blood group. If a suitable donor is unavailable one experiences indescribable anxiety and agony.

Wealth

Most fail to fulfil this wish despite their untiring efforts. One feels unhappy when one makes a bad investment, when interest rates decline, when the stock market takes a dive, and when one does not win the lottery. Some attempt to "peep" into the future to identify "opportunities for wealth and luck" through astrology, palmistry, crystal ball gazing, and geomancy.

Happiness

Everyone tries to find happiness in accordance with their individual conceptions of happiness. Most people identify happiness with the gratification of sensual desire, but sensual desire is insatiable and hence in the end the pursuit of sensual pleasures only brings suffering.

Others view as the source of happiness the acquisition of wealth and property, or personal success in their professional careers, or the achievement of fame and repute. Such aims, however, cannot always be realized. When we fail to achieve them we feel frustrated and upset. But even when we succeed, such attainments cannot last forever, and thus when they slip away from us we are left feeling dejected and depressed.

Relationships

One cannot find the ideal life-partner despite one's efforts; married couples who wish to have children cannot do so; or when they have children, the children are not of their preferred sex.

One's love for another is unrequitted.

One children are unfilial.

Insecurity

Many are insecure regarding their basic needs such as food, clothing, shelter, and medicine.

Others feel insecure regarding their job, especially in a job-scarce environment, or on account of such financial conditions as inflation or recession.

Still others, who live in an societies plagued by war, riots, and looting, must worry about their physical safety.

Basic abilities

The blind wish to see, the deaf to hear, the dumb to speak, the lame to walk, the bedridden paralytic to move around again. Yet because they cannot fulfil these wishes, they experience disappointment and suffering.

In what way is *the composite body* itself a cause of suffering?

It is a cause of suffering because one constantly and continually must protect it from hunger, thirst, and changing climatic conditions; keep it healthy by regular exercise; keep it clean by washing, bathing, and excretion; keep it neat and tidy by trimming one's nails and cutting one's hair.

It is also a cause of suffering because in the end, despite all our efforts, it succumbs to old age, illness, and death.

III
Analysis of Anattā

What is the meaning of the word "*anattā*"?
The Pali word "*anattā*" is often translated as non-self, non-ego, egolessness, impersonality, and substancelessness.

What is substanceless?
One is oneself substanceless, and all conditioned things around one are substanceless.

In what way is one substanceless oneself?
The human being is actually a combination of material and mental phenomena classified into five categories or "aggregates." These are:

form
feeling
perception
mental formations
consciousness.

Of these, form is material, and the other four are mental phenomena.

How does one regard *material phenomena* as the self?

The body (as a whole) is regarded as "I" and "mine"

When we think, "I sit," "I walk," "I stand," "I lie down," we take the whole body, by way of its posture, to be "I."

When we think, "My height is 1.8 metres," we take the whole body, by way of its dimensions, to be "mine."

Ironically, without a mirror, we cannot even see our whole head, neck, or back, yet we claim that our body is our self. Even what we see in the mirror is just a *reflection* of the body, not the real thing.

Individual parts of the body are regarded as "I" and "mine"

Some examples:

"My hair is shiny": an attached body part (the hair on the head) is taken to be "mine."

"I like to touch silk": an attached body part (the skin on the palm and fingers) is taken to be "I."

"Oops! A strand of my hair has fallen into the soup!": a detached body part (a strand of hair) is taken to be "mine."

"I am sending my urine sample to the laboratory for analysis": a detached body part (urine) is taken to be "mine."

How does one regard *mental phenomena* as the self?

Contact between sense base and sense object being regarded as "I"

Example: eyes + visible form: "I saw a rainbow."

Implication: sense base (eyes) = "I"

This example is applicable to the other sense bases: ear, nose, tongue, and body.

Feeling that arises through such contact being regarded as "I"
Example: (skin of) whole body + tactile object (cold air):
"I feel cold in here."
Implication: unpleasant bodily feeling = "I"

Example: eyes + visible form, *combined with* ears + sound:
"I like this movie."
Implication: pleasant feeling = "I"

States of mind being regarded as "I"
Example: "I felt very restless this morning."
Implication: mental state (restlessness) = "I"
Example: "I feel guilty about visiting her so seldom."
Implication: mental state (guilty conscience) = "I"
Example: "I was worried that you wouldn't come back."
Implication: mental state (worry) = "I"

Objects being regarded as "mine"

Tangible objects
Example: "My dentures are getting loose."
Implication: tangible object attached to body (dentures) =
"mine"
Example: "This is my car."
Implication: tangible object not attached to body (car) =
"mine"

Intangible objects
Example: "After the race, my energy is drained."
Implication: intangible object pertaining to body (i.e.,
energy) = "mine"
Example: "I've achieved only half of what I'd hoped to
do."

Implication: intangible object not pertaining to body (achievement) = "mine"

Example: "His words hurt my pride."

Implication: intangible object not pertaining to body (self-respect) = "mine"

Example: "I'm reputed to be a responsible person."

Implication: intangible object not pertaining to body (reputation) = "mine"

One's attributes being regarded as "I", "me" and "mine"

Example: "I was so embarrassed."

Implication: attribute (self-esteem) = "I"

Example: "I'm afraid of snakes."

Implication: attribute (fear) = "I"

Example: "I can sing English songs."

Implication: attribute (ability) = "I"

Example: "I'm a teacher."

Implication: attribute (occupation) = "I"

Example: "I'm twenty years old."

Implication: attribute (age) = "I"

Example: "I'm a man," "I'm a woman."

Implication: attribute (gender) = "I"

Example: "That's me in the photograph!"

Implication: attribute (printed image of body) = "me"

Example: "That's me in the mirror."

Implication: attribute (reflected image of one's body) = "me"

Example: "I left my body warmth on that seat."

Implication: attribute (conducted warmth) = "mine"

Example: "That's an insult to my intelligence."

Implication: attribute (intelligence) = "mine"

Example: "My memory is not as good as yours."

Implication: attribute (memory) = "mine"
Example: "My name is Paul."
Implication: attribute (name) = "mine"

Regarding one's associates as "mine"
Example: "This is my father."
Implication: father = "mine"
Example: "This is my wife/husband; those are my children."
Implication: wife/husband and children = "mine"

In what way are *all conditioned things* around oneself substanceless?

1. All conditioned things that we perceive through our senses are in reality *not what they appear to be* for the following reasons:

The limitations of our senses
We come into contact with things around us through the five physical sense bases, namely the eyes, ears, nose, tongue and the body. We conceive all phenomena through the mind base.

However, what we see with our eyes represents only a small segment of the spectrum of electromagnetic rays, for the optic nerves of humans are sensitive only to waves with lengths ranging from around 400 to 700 mu. Those waves that are present but outside this range – such as infrared rays, ultraviolet rays, and X-rays – are invisible to us.

Likewise we can hear only sound waves that are within the sound spectrum of humans. Such limitations apply to the nose, tongue and the mind as well.

Language

General concepts

It is generally acceptable to say, "The sun rises in the east and sets in the west." In actuality, however, the sun neither rises nor sets. The earth merely revolves on its axis relative to the sun. The so-called "sunrise" of one continent is the "sunset" of another. In this context is it possible to locate the exact position of the horizon? Can one touch a rainbow?

The composite nature of things

When the component parts of a thing are separated, the thing loses its identity and assumes another. For example, when a car is dismantled the concept "car" disappears and its identity is replaced by "bumper," "windscreen," "steering wheel," "tyre," and so forth.

A chopped-up pig is known as "pork."

A flattened carton is called cardboard.

There are also cases where the identity of a thing changes even without the apparent separation of its constituent parts. For example, when a person dies the concept "man" is replaced by that of "corpse."

State of flux

It is not possible to step into the "same" river twice since its waters are ever changing.

From moment to moment the flame of a candle is neither the same nor totally different.

Advancements in science and technology

A film show appears real enough to invoke passions, but in reality it is merely a display of images produced by light and accompanied by sound.

An event recorded on a video-camera appears to be real, but what happens if one replays it in reverse order? One will see a recorded event that has never taken place!

By using photo-imaging software to modify a photograph taken with a digital camera, one can portray oneself standing on the peak of Mount Everest – clad only in swimwear!

One can produce a show depicting oneself dancing with a cartoon figure like Mickey Mouse or appear to act alongside film stars who have long been dead.

The virtual infant "Cha-Cha," who displays lifelike bodily movements, is actually a 3-D animation package created by a computer artist by applying realistic human movement to a digitally created character.

In the virtual reality system MIRAGE (Modelling and Immersion in Realtime Advanced Graphics Environment), one simply needs to put on a pair of 3-D goggles to "walk through" a building, decide on its interior decor and colour schemes, even how the furniture is positioned, before the building is built.

Likewise, without leaving one's study, one can "explore" the tombs of the pharaoh of Egypt with convincingly true-to-life sights and sounds.

The voice of someone who does not even exist can be generated by means of a voice synthesizer.

By animatronics one can produce a thrilling show of computer graphics.

In the Virtual Aquarium, video images are used to re-create swimming fish with special filming technology and lighting.

2. Conditioned things *do not possess a fixed substantial nature* due to their dual aspects.

General characteristics

Brightness and darkness

The moment the door is opened on to a pitch-dark room, darkness instantly disappears and is replaced by light. This leaves an interesting question: Where does the darkness go, and where does the brightness come from?

Light and heavy

These characteristics are relative. An object considered "light" in comparison with something heavier than itself may be "heavy" when compared with something else lighter than itself.

These characteristics are also subject-dependent. An object considered "light" by a young adult is experienced as heavy by children and the elderly.

Cold and hot

A day when the temperature is 55° F will be experienced as cool in early autumn but as warm in early spring. A beverage of the same temperature will be experienced as cool if it is tea but as warm if it is lemonade.

Cleanliness and dirtiness

Upon comparison, what is deemed clean by us will be dirty to a surgeon about to perform a critical operation. One's body is considered clean immediately after a shower. After a period of time, it is deemed dirty again. One may ask: At precisely which point in time does cleanliness turn into dirtiness?

We can apply the same consideration to: youth and old age; the blooming and withering of flowers; the freshness and staleness of food; hunger and satiation; slow motion and fast motion; the present, past and future.

Things undergo changes, not only with the passage of time, but also in relation to space. Some space-dependent relative characteristics are:

> near and far;
> low and high;
> long and short.

Examples can be multiplied ad infinitum. Work out the implications for yourselves.

Conclusion

You may ask: How do the three characteristics relate to one another?

Before we answer this question, it is timely to analyse what we regard as happiness.

Generally, happiness can be classified under the following headings:

1. *Gratification of sensual desires*

That is, the happiness that comes from seeing pleasant objects, hearing pleasant sounds, smelling pleasant odours, tasting pleasant flavours, touching pleasant surfaces, and entertaining pleasant thoughts.

2. *Being healthy and vigorous*

It is only when one is healthy and strong that one can enjoy sensual pleasures and embark on any activity that one finds pleasurable.

3. *Being youthful (or attractive)*

This enables one to enjoy feeling superior to others and to enjoy their admiration (and sometimes their envy).

4. *Having pleasant relationships*

This includes having a happy family life, true friends, and pleasant colleagues. One feels happy when the love or concern one showers on others is requitted.

5. *Having high social status*

For some this is relative to the quality and quantity of their possessions.

Others regard high education as a status symbol.

The happiness is derived from feeling superior to others or from winning their admiration (and sometimes their envy).

6. *Being famous or renowned*

One enjoys being known, recognized, and admired by others.

7. *Being powerful*

One enjoys having others at one's disposal.

8. *Being safe and secure*

One feels happy when one is not in debt; has no worry about food, clothing, shelter, and medicine; has a stable job and lives in a peaceful country.

Most of the above goods can be acquired by wealth. Thus wealth seems to be the main basis of happiness.

Now let us return to the question: How do the three characteristics relate to one another?

Impermanence leads to suffering

Impermanence leads to suffering because that which we regard as a source of happiness does not last forever. Whatever in the world we turn to as a source of happiness will inevitably be overrun by aging, decay, death, and destruction.

Why are we often moved to tears when we flip through old photo albums, listen to songs from the "good old days," watch a show one had seen long ago, touch objects of sentimental value, or visit places pertaining to one's childhood or youth? The reason is that we are still attached to the sentiments (happiness included) we experienced at that time, which we are not able to bring back! We have aged, and so have the people at that time. Some may have died, while children have grown into adults. Places and objects have changed or no longer exist. Those events cannot be repeated.

As soon as they pass, events that bring happiness lead to suffering. That explains the "down" feeling which some experience when their holiday comes to an end. Those "encore cries" at the end of an emotionally-charged concert can be attributed to this too.

Present suffering exists due to the belief in a self

We are conditioned from the time of birth to regard things that are really substanceless as possessing a self or substantial nature.

By positing a real self, we draw a line to demarcate that which is self from that which is not self but surrounds the self. Being ignorant of the fact that all things around the self are also substanceless, we categorize them into the pleasant, the unpleasant, and the neutral.

By clinging to the notion that there is a self which "feels," "enjoys," and "suffers," we desire the pleasant and detest the unpleasant. When the pleasant changes, we suffer. By not understanding that the unpleasant is also ever-changing, we suffer too when we are exposed to unpleasant conditions.

Our belief in the self is reinforced when others shower praise on us or when we achieve recognition. These tendencies condition our perceptions and influence our thoughts, words, and deeds.

In reality, the "enjoyment" and "suffering" are merely our responses to the feelings that arise when our senses contact their respective sense objects. The self that "feels" is merely the arisen feeling.

Believing that the self exists leads to future suffering

By responding to a pleasurable feeling (caused by a pleasant sense object) with *desire*, kamma is accumulated.

Likewise, by responding to an unpleasant feeling (caused by an unpleasant sense object) with *repulsion*, kamma is also accumulated.

Kamma is rooted in our ignorance about the three characteristics. As long as ignorance about the three characteristics remains, when the present life comes to an end, one must undergo rebirth. Rebirth entails the whole mass of suffering (*dukkha*).

Certain schools of thought argue that "suffering makes us mature," that we should "learn to appreciate love," that "tough times build character," that "turmoil can toughen people," that "pain warns us of danger," and so on.

It is not my intention here to discuss the necessity or purpose of suffering in human life; nor do I wish to paint a seemingly "pessimistic" picture of life. My aim is only to review life's stark realities, which many people take for granted.

To understand this point, one need only answer this question honestly and without prejudice : "Do I suffer?"

At this juncture of understanding the three characteristics of existence intellectually, what can we do to improve on the situation? We should strive ardently to realize their existence in all our day-to-day activities.

The following are some suggestions:

To realize impermanence
Be more sensitive towards the changes that occur to and within one's body.

Always be aware of the changes that occur in one's thoughts, feelings, and opinions.

Maintain keen observation of the changing nature of all the things and events around oneself.

To realize suffering
Identify the type of suffering one is experiencing whenever some type of suffering arises.

To realize selflessness
Contemplate one's body and see clearly that the body, being an object of cognition, cannot properly be considered one's self.

Be aware of one's mental reactions when any of the senses contacts its respective sense object. See that because these mental phenomena are conditioned by a sense faculty and objects, they cannot be a substantial self.

See that the things around one are devoid of any "substance" or "entity." Reflect on their impermanence, and see that because they are impermanent they cannot be taken as substantial, self-subsistent realities.

See that these things are dependent for their existence and sustenance on their own proper conditions, and thus lack the independence of conditions essential to the concept of substance.

The Buddha has given a detailed exposition on this practical aspect of training in the Discourse on the Foundations of Mindfulness (Satipatthāna Sutta). By ardently establishing these four foundations of mindfulness, one will eventually realize that all phenomena are merely physical and mental processess.

They arise due to other supportive conditions. Those supportive conditions also arise due to some other supportive conditions. They are ever-changing and do not possess any unchanging entity of their own.

This wisdom will transform our thoughts, words, and deeds. Eventually it will free us from the cycle of birth and death, bringing us to the ultimate end of suffering: that which is permanent, ever blissful, and beyond causes and conditions—Nibbāna.

The Seven Contemplations of Insight

Prepared under the guidance of
Ven. Mātara Sri Ñānārāma Mahāthera

The present book evolved out of a series of discourses on the "eighteen principal insights" that the Venerable Mātara Sri Ñānārāma Mahāthera gave in 1981 to the meditating monks at his monastery, the Nissarana Vanaya Hermitage, in Mitirigala, Sri Lanka. Prepared by a pupil of Ven Ñānārāma under his personal guidance, this book offers the reader an in-depth study of the first seven insights, which form a distinct and self-sufficient system known as "the seven contemplations" (*satta anupassanā*). At once theoretically rigorous yet pragmatic and precise, the book weaves together extensive material from the Buddha's discourses and the commentaries with concrete guidelines to mental training. By giving us a vivid picture of how these seven contemplations are to be applied in the actual course of meditation practice, this work serves to fill a major gap in our understanding of Buddhist insight meditation.

THE BUDDHIST PUBLICATION SOCIETY

The BPS is an approved charity dedicated to making known the Teaching of the Buddha, which has a vital message for people of all creeds. Founded in 1958, the BPS has published a wide variety of books and booklets covering a great range of topics. Its publications include accurate annotated translations of the Buddha's discourses, standard reference works, as well as original contemporary expositions of Buddhist thought and practice. These works present Buddhism as it truly is—a dynamic force which has influenced receptive minds for the past 2500 years and is still as relevant today as it was when it first arose. A full list of our publications will be sent upon request. Write to:

The Hony. Secretary
BUDDHIST PUBLICATION SOCIETY
P.O. Box 61
54, Sangharaja Mawatha
Kandy • Sri Lanka
E–mail: bps@mail.lanka.net
Website: http://www.lanka.com/dhamma